A Suspect Culture a
production in associa

C000264664

STATIC

A story of love, loss and compilation tapes

By Dan Rebellato

A Suspect Culture and Graeae Theatre Company
production in association with Tron Theatre, Glasgow

STATIC

A story of love, loss and compilation tapes

By Dan Rebellato

Static was first produced by Suspect Culture and Graeae Theatre
Company and presented at Tron Theatre, Glasgow on 20 February 2008

GLASGOW Tron Theatre, EDINBURGH The Traverse, STIRLING Macrobert,
INVERNESS Eden Court, NEWCASTLE Northern Stage,
MANCHESTER Contact, PLYMOUTH The Drum, BELFAST Baby Grand,
BIRMINGHAM Birmingham Repertory Theatre, LONDON Soho Theatre

www.suspectculture.com/**static**   www.graeae.org/**static**

CAST
In order of speaking

Chris **Steven Webb**
Julia **Jeni Draper**
Martin **Tom Thomasson**
Sarah **Pauline Lockhart**

CREATIVE TEAM

Writer **Dan Rebellato**
Directors **Graham Eatough and Jenny Sealey**
Design **Ian Scott**
Sound **Kenny MacLeod**

PRODUCTION TEAM

Production Manager **Jools Walls**
Company Stage Manager **Vicky Wilson**
Technical Stage Manager **Maria Bechaalani**
Design Assistant **Claire Halleran**
Sign Language Interpreters **Andy Long and Natalie MacDonald**
Access Workers **Jeffrey Lamont and Jenny Mullin**
Access Consultants **Sally Clay and Kat Fisher**

Marketing Manager for *Static* **Jeni Iannetta**
Press Manager for *Static* **David Burns, Burning Issues PR**
Publicity Design **Frozen River**

SUSPECT CULTURE

Artistic Director **Graham Eatough**
General Manager **David Morgan**
Interpretation Officer **Devina Kumar**
Administrator **Judith Riddell**
Finance Officer **Brian Daly**

Board of Directors
Hugh Hodgart, Jeni Iannetta, Jim Law, Jack Queen, David Williams

Associate Artists
Renato Gabrielli, David Greig, Andrés Lima, Patrick Macklin, Maurício Paroni de Castro, Nick Powell, Dan Rebellato, Sergio Romano, Ian Scott

GRAEAE

Artistic Director **Jenny Sealey**
Executive Director **Judith Kilvington**
Access and HR Director **Claire Saddleton**
General Manager **Kevin Walsh**
Finance Manager **Kudzai Mushangwe**
Training and Learning Projects Manager **Rachel Bagshaw**
Literary Manager **Alex Bulmer**
Scene Change Co-ordinator **Nicole Stoute**
Access Support Assistant **Michael Achtman**
Temporary Administrative Assistant **Claudia Elmhirst**
Finance Consultant **Barbara Simmonds**

Board of Directors
Emma Dunton, Avis Johns, Steve Mannix, Steve Moffitt, Jodi Myers, Theresa Veith

Associate Artists
Jamie Beddard, Mandy Colleran, David Ellington, Tim Gebbels, Kaz Langley, Nicola Miles-Wildin, Sophie Partridge, Amit Sharma, Nicole Stoute, Donal Toolan, David Toole

THANKS

Conrad Brunström, Marjory Carnegie, Caroline Conlon, Iñigo Garrido, Sebastian Gorton, Cherylee Houston, Mike Kenny, Andy Long, Lizzie Malcolm, Radha Manjeshwar, Jo Masson, Maxwell McCarthy, Linda McLean, Jim McSharry, Gaelle Mellis, Donna Mullings, Pickles Norman, Malcolm Rogan, Scott Associates, Amit Sharma, Billy Smart, Robert Softley, Lucy Taylor, David Toole, Carole Williams, Kevin Wratten

Biographies

Jeni Draper performer
Jeni trained at Webber Douglas and has worked nationally and internationally for many companies both on TV and in theatre, most recently in Jenny Sealey's production of *Blood Wedding* in Tokyo. She regularly interprets shows at The Almeida, Soho Theatre and Queen's Hornchurch amongst others. Jeni is a co-founder of The Fingersmiths Ltd, a company dedicated to exploring the theatrical possibilities of BSL with spoken and written English.

Gig you wish you'd been to *Bob Marley Lyceum Theatre July 19th 1975 London*
What gets you dancing? *Scissor Sisters 'I don't feel like dancin'*

Graham Eatough director
Graham co-founded Suspect Culture in 1992 and has been the company's artistic director since 1995. He has been involved in all Suspect Culture's productions and has also directed work for the Tron Theatre, 7:84 and Cryptic Productions. Graham has directed short film with the Film Council's Digicult Project, and has worked as a performer in film, television and theatre. He received a Creative Scotland Award in 2001.

Gig you wish you'd been to *The Last Waltz by The Band and The Smiths at The Hacienda*
What gets you dancing? *Northern Soul*

Pauline Lockhart performer
Pauline's theatre work includes productions with National Theatre of Scotland, Royal Lyceum Edinburgh, Improbable Theatre, Manchester Royal Exchange, West Yorkshire Playhouse, and Hampstead Theatre. Her TV and Film credits include *Monarch of the Glen*, *Holby City*, *Casualty*, *The Glass*, *Heartless*, *Strictly Sinatra*, and *Gladiatress*. She has won the Best Supporting Actress award by Theatrical Management Association and the Manchester Evening News award.

Gig you wish you'd been to *The Velvet Underground at The Factory, New York*
What gets you dancing? *Something funky like James Brown or just fun like The Scissor Sisters*

Kenny MacLeod sound designer

Kenny is an audio engineer / producer and software developer based in Glasgow. Currently working as production manager at Glasgow's Centre for Contemporary Arts (CCA), he is involved in the production and development of a range of art forms. As a sound designer and engineer Kenny has worked internationally with a range of theatre, performance and record companies.

Gig you wish you'd been to *Drive like jehu / chavez / Heavy Vegetable*
What gets you dancing? *Richie Hawtin*

Ian Scott designer

After working on Airport in 1996, Ian joined Suspect Culture as an Associate Artist. He designed the set and lighting for *Timeless* (1997) and *Mainstream* (1999) and has worked on many of Suspect Culture's subsequent shows. Ian has also collaborated on a number of Graeae productions, most recently *Blasted* (2007). Other current projects include *Our Friends in the North* (Northern Stage), *The 39 Steps* (Criterion Theatre) and *Duck!* (Unicorn).

Gig you wish you'd been to *Cud reunion tour (2006)*
What gets you dancing? *'Ain't Nobody' - Chaka Khan*

Jenny Sealey director

Jenny has been director of Graeae since 1997. Her recent work includes *Blasted* by Sarah Kane, *Whiter than Snow* by Mike Kenny (co-production with Birmingham Repertory Theatre) and *Flower Girls* by Richard Cameron (co-production with New Wolsey Theatre). Most recently she has worked on *Blood Wedding* at Tram Theatre, Tokyo. Jenny lives with her partner Danny Braverman and 13 year old son, Jonah.

Gig you wish you'd been to *I would love to have seen Jimi Hendrix, The Doors, Bob Marley. The Clash. The list is endless.*
What gets you dancing? *Patti Smith*

Dan Rebellato writer

Dan's plays include *Mile End, Here's What I Did With My Body One Day, Chekhov in Hell, A Modest Adjustment* and *Outright Terror Bold and Brilliant*. He co-wrote (with David Greig) *Futurology* for Suspect Culture. His work for radio includes *Erskine May, Emily Rising, Cavalry*, and adaptations of *The Midwich Cuckoos, Dead Souls* and *Girlfriend in a Coma*.

Gig you wish you'd been to *The Ramones at The Rainbow, London, New Year's Eve 1977. But seeing Dylan go 'electric' at the Newport Folk Festival in 1965 would have been pretty great. Beatles rooftop gig? Wish I'd seen Nirvana.*
What gets you dancing? *Cajun music, Western Swing, or Girls Aloud. Nothing else: I'm a purist.*

Tom Thomasson performer

Tom has performed with Graeae previously on their tour of *Whiter Than Snow* and is part of Theatre Active's pool of performers. Tom also works as a drama facilitator and has recently been delivering workshops for Kazzum. He is a freelancer for organisations such as the Half Moon Theatre Company and also enjoys supporting the StopGap Dance Company in their education programmes.

Gig you wish you'd been to *I wish I had been to the Crowded House 'farewell to the world' gig at the Sydney Opera house. It would have been great to see them perform in Australia!*
What gets you dancing? *I love Superstition by Stevie Wonder almost as much as Stevie probably does.*

Steven Webb performer

Steven has worked as an actor, director, writer and workshop co-ordinator/ facilitator over the past 10 years. He graduated from Reading University with a degree in theatre studies and has a BTEC in National Performing Arts from Barking College. As well as his work in theatre Steven has performed in *Switch* (BBC2) and *Rush* (Channel 4). He was one of the co-founders of Deafinitely Theatre, a professional Deaf-led theatre company, and he co-founded DRoots in 2007, a Deaf youth/ children's theatre company.

Gig you wish you'd been to *Actually, I never thought of it*
What gets you dancing? *Anything apart from R&B music, never able to get into it.*

Steven Webb (top) and Pauline Lockhart (bottom) during *Static* rehearsals at Tron Theatre, Glasgow.

Photography: Lizzie Malcolm

Suspect Culture

Suspect Culture is an artistically driven contemporary arts organisation based in Glasgow. We create new performance work in a variety of media; primarily theatre but also visual art and film. All our activity is based on a set of core values:

Collaboration

- we are committed to sharing artistic visions with a wide variety of leading artists and organisations supporting them in developing skills and fulfilling potential. We create work through a rigorous collaborative process involving extensive development periods including research, workshops and experimentation

Interdisciplinarity

- we explore performance in a variety of contexts with leading artists from different disciplines. We want to explore these different formats to enrich our audience's relationship with the company and its work

Internationalism

- we maintain relationships with associate artists from a variety of countries, exchanging different cultural influences and creative approaches which directly influence the content of our work

Interpretation

- we create engaging interpretive materials and events, enhancing our audience's experience of our work

We are committed to offering an ideal environment for artists to unlock their creative potential and make high quality work for a range of audiences.

Lines of Enquiry

Extract from recorded conversation with Graham Eatough, artistic director of Suspect Culture, on *Static*.

Max: How does Static connect with Suspect Culture's previous work?

Graham: *Static* is both different and the same as our previous work. There are *key* differences and the most obvious one is its use of sign language and a deaf performer and the fact that it's being co-directed by Jenny Sealey, who is partially deaf. They are key differences but in an interesting way they're also extensions of work that Suspect Culture has been very interested in, in the past. And I suppose this revolves around certain key themes that have cropped up in our shows over the past 12 years, which very loosely are about the ways in which people try and communicate with each other. The ways in which these often lead to failure or misunderstanding, or that the successes we have in trying to communicate emotions to each other might be accidental or slightly out-with our control. So maybe it's the way we physically communicate that really tells the truth about what we feel, rather than our words. Maybe it's the mistakes made whilst we're speaking, what we let slip by accident.

These kinds of issues have been really interesting to us for a long time now and it's why we've worked a lot with different languages. In the past we've worked with Italian, Spanish and Portuguese (*Airport* 1995, *The Golden Ass* 1999). In the case of a play like *A Different Language* (2005), which was half in Italian, half English, it was purposefully designed so that the audiences' *not understanding* of half of the dialogue wouldn't be a barrier to their enjoyment or their overall engagement with the play. And setting yourself that challenge obviously raises really interesting issues around, say, physical communication or what somebody's emotions communicate beyond language.

The other element that's been significant in relation to *Static* from previous work has been a physical approach that Suspect Culture has had. We've tried over the years to develop a performance style which isn't wholly naturalistic; which has often involved gesture and a kind of precision to the physicality – a choreography I suppose, in some kind of minimal way. And that's been very important to us and has led us to create work where actors would be required to perform things that probably *did* look a bit like sign – whether they're character gestures or gestures that somehow speak of a given emotion behind a conversation, for example.

Static also connects in a really interesting way with the short film *Missing* we made last year. Both pieces deal with loss and the way the mind works to cope with loss. In the case of *Missing* it's about a woman whose husband has disappeared and her fantasy of him coming home, and we represented that fantasy on screen. With *Static* there's a similar representation at work in the form of Chris, who's recently died, but who appears on stage throughout. Both portrayals allow us to explore the grieving process and how, to those left behind, the deceased or lost can still have an overwhelming presence even after they've physically gone.

All of these strands of work seem to connect really directly with what we've done with *Static*. It's very satisfying to see us deepening our exploration of these lines of enquiry in this exciting new way.

[Interview by work placement student Maxwell McCarthy from Royal Scottish Academy of Music and Drama]

Graeae

Graeae's artistic vision exploits the ambition the company has for its staff, artists and creative partners. The vision comprises four key elements:

- a diversity of plays written by disabled and non disabled writers to enable us to cover the broad spectrum of theatre and the language of performance

- a diversity of education models to act as a catalyst to inspire the creativity of a new generation of theatre makers

- the development of comprehensive barrier free performance, writing and technical training opportunities to inform a lasting legacy of Deaf and disabled people as a body of talent to be employed across the creative industry

- exploration of the aesthetics of access to inform theatre as a whole experience for both creators and audiences

Graeae's artistic plans are always informed by the company's mission to achieve equality of opportunity for disabled people working in all aspects of professional theatre.

Graeae now finds itself heralded as a pioneering company which is hard to 'pigeon hole' because of the wide diversity of styles and practices its work encompasses.

The company's understanding of 'accessible diversity', cultural diversity and diversity of theatrical style inform and permeate every aspect of the artistic plan and the company ethos.

Every Seventh Word

Jenny Sealey, artistic director of Graeae, on her experience of music

Graham and I met at a party during the Edinburgh Festival in 2003. We started chatting about Suspect Culture's show *One, Two…* and how, because I generally hear one in seven words, I had made up my own word/ sound-scape of this show. And so began the courtship between Suspect Culture and Graeae and the development of *Static*. We discovered that both companies shared an interest in the diverse expanse and minutiae of communication, and what happens in the misunderstanding, mishearing or misinterpreting of spoken or signed language.

The emotional landscape of *Static* impacts on us all as love and loss cement human beings and allow us to share a common parlance. Placing music in the equation gives us another commonly used tool to unravel the emotional density of loss, which is so personal and individual.

Music takes me out of my comfort zone. I have an odd, eclectic taste in music based entirely on whether I can hear one or two lines of the lyrics or not. Or sometimes I will love the tune and have no idea what the song is, only to be told it is something dire and laughable and no one in their right mind would like it.

In September 2007 my partner bought me a flat headphone contraption which fits behind my ear and allows me to use the T switch on my hearing aid to access music from an iPod. I was completely unprepared for the sheer overwhelming wave of emotion that swept over me and I dived under the duvet and bawled my eyes out. I could access music (and some words) in a way I have never been able to before (and I have an iPod).

Music is now a much bigger part of some deaf people's lives through new technology, but how do we convey the presence of music to those who will never hear it? The physicality of *Static*, the rhythm of the movement, signs and gestures are all part of a musical landscape which requires no sound. At the same time the heard landscape needs to resonate emotionally and create a clear visual picture in the minds of people who are blind and visually impaired. The result of our exploration is a play with multiple and diverse communication strands.

Static has remained truly faithful to the concept of every seventh word. The deliberate eclectic gaps within the narrative and layering of different styles of communication creates a space to allow the audience to fill the gaps, deconstruct the layers and own their personal emotional map of the play.

Static Set

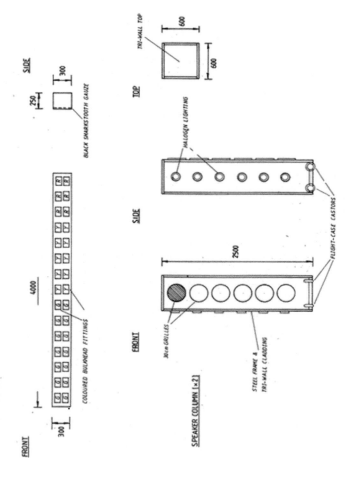

LIGHTBOX / PROJECTION SCREEN (FLOWN)

FRONT

SIDE

4000

300

250

300

COLOURED BULKHEAD FITTINGS

BLACK SHARKSTOOTH GAUZE

SPEAKER COLUMN (x2)

FRONT

SIDE

TOP

TRI-WALL TOP

600

600

2500

HALOGEN LIGHTING

FLIGHT-CASE CASTORS

30cm GRILLES

STEEL FRAME &
TRI-WALL CLADDING

Notes on Design

Ian Scott

Three stations
Reflective space between – static
Two towers of sound and light
Light as sound
Sign as sound
A band stage
Warm - varnished walnut
Something lasting
A studio
Recording/ remembering
Resolutely retro
Analogue's the future…
Sometimes only a cliché will do
A slight delay - static
A big hug
A home

The Brilliant Moment

Stephen McRobbie, a member of Glasgow-based independent music pioneers, The Pastels

I am twelve years old and I want to take control of an important part of my life. I am an only child and I feel I am already controlling some things okay but there's other randomness which I would ideally like to eliminate. Amongst these random things are songs I don't like which come on the radio or television. I want to accentuate the positive, to concentrate on the brilliant things all the time, to somehow replay over and over something which is for me a brilliant sound, a brilliant piece of music. I manage to persuade my parents that a Phillips EL3302 cassette recorder (with condenser mic) is an affordable option with practical benefits.

Initially I want to be able to make a little moment for myself, or even better a series of little moments which can expand into a bigger moment. I don't think I want to set a limit on this bigger moment but my parents, more experienced with the scale of things, provide me with a C60 (30 minutes a side). Initial experiments with mic and television throw up problems with background noise / interruption and although I really love my Phillips EL3302 I realise that it is not the complete answer to my needs and I slowly drift off into a new world of building my own record collection, although out of loyalty I occasionally buy (or am given) some pre-recorded cassette like a weird Italian Beatles compilation.

After a few years the two worlds spectacularly collide into a 'music-system' and I am at last ready to realise my younger hopes for a more compiled lifestyle. With hindsight I realise that these forays into compilation tapes adhered to my earlier philosophy of one brilliant sound after the other as I strived for some kind of consistent excellence with no real ebb and flow. This very much corresponded with what I felt was the most interesting music of the early 1980s as represented by post-punk and DIY singles or recordings from the radio of John Peel sessions. By now I am making music too with my group, The Pastels, and I pass on tapes to group members and friends with compiled 'other stuff'. I get tapes back and suddenly I'm hearing all kinds of new things, related but sometimes slightly random – that was okay.

We came to know things about each other, not just the music. I don't know if we were trying to pass on messages through our tape making but it felt very direct and personal, the sound of the pause button and some speedy graphic art. Technically they became better too, as we familiarised ourselves with the best makes and learnt how hot we could go. I know I always thought of the person that I was making the tape for and tried to make it a perfect tape even when in my heart I knew that something imperfect was better. Now I feel some of these older tapes are like polaroids - mysterious, pale moments which out of context seem awkward or faded, but occasionally the colour is a more vivid hue and once again they are exactly the brilliant moment.

Chris's Promise

I would pull up the roots of the earth
I would pluck the stars from the sky
I would swim through oceans of my tears
I would ride a thousand wild horses
I would revisit the battlefields
I would balance on the top of the world
I would run from the edge of the earth
I would reach to the depths of my heart
I would walk among sunspots
I would crawl through my worst memories
I would sail through nightmares
I would walk ten thousand miles in the mouth of a graveyard
I would exhume the mass graves
I would eat iron and drink barbed wire
For another minute with you

White Noise / Empty Rooms

Dan Rebellato

John Peel once said of his own death that one of his big regrets would be that he wouldn't get to hear the next album by The Fall. A few years ago, I played The Magnetic Fields' *69 Love Songs* to a mate of mine who visibly mourned again a friend who would never now hear it. An old schoolfriend of mine had to attend that most terrible of occasions: the funeral of his own child. During the drinks afterwards, he tired of the tasteful music and discovered that only a truly gaudy song – in this instance William Shatner's cover of 'Common People' – could release the emotions and allow them to mourn.

We live with music and music outlives us. Pop music's talent for renewal and rebirth would be an affront to the mute finality of death if it weren't so generous. Music offers itself out, reaches right into us. The bands and songs and singers I've loved aren't just adornments to my life, they're part of it. Who would I be without The Smiths? If I'd never heard Gorky's Zygotic Mynci? If I'd never encountered Iris Dement or Nirvana or Belle and Sebastian? I don't know that person.

Hearing a song I love I have a whole-body response to it. Just yesterday, listening to The Okkervil River's 'A Girl in Port', I find myself not just mentally stimulated, but physically breathless with pleasure, a shiver runs right through me on the final verse, and as the exultantly sad pedal steel takes over from the horns my eyes brim with real tears.

But it intrigues me that these experiences don't stay private. Music is generous and it makes us generous too. We hear a song we like and we tell our friends, we text our friends, we stick it on a compilation and wait for their response, we say *you have to listen to this* and hand over the headphones. Liking music isn't private, it extends out from ourselves, we want to share it. Music is not just a way of connecting people; our relationships with music are somewhat *like* the relationships we have with other people. It's no surprise that we mourn the music we won't hear.

I freely admit to not understanding death. What does it mean if someone was here yesterday and not here today? No wonder we invented the soul. I am struck by the central image of Joan Didion's *The Year of Magical Thinking*. I don't believe in ghosts or an afterlife or a spirit world or séances. But I think I understand the way they swoop in to fill a gap in our understanding of the world. Death remains such a mystery, seems so unthinkable in the mind of the living, that isn't any attempt to think death kind of magical?

When Jenny Sealey, Graham Eatough and I first started working with Sign, I watched, as a non-Signer, an abstract series of movements which sometimes form themselves into a shape I recognise or guess. Meaning suddenly piercing the chaos. Sometimes in my effort to understand what was being signed I 'saw' whole sentences that weren't really there. It reminded me of those people who hear, in a tape recording of an empty room, out of the white noise, the consoling voice of a deceased friend.

It also reminded me of my teenage self, rewinding the tape again and again to decipher a muffled lyric, or playing tapes of bootlegged decade-old Buzzcocks gigs from the 1970s, rendered almost inaudible by multi-generation copying, and the effort of listening, of wanting to hear, that brought perhaps illusory but still satisfying shape and meaning to something long gone.

I wanted *Static* to explore this territory: this delicate area of failed prayer and creative listening, of death and dancing, gigs and grief, of the things that come between us and the things that invisibly connect us.

STATIC

First published in 2008 by Oberon Books Ltd

521 Caledonian Road, London N7 9RH

Tel: 020 7607 3637 / Fax: 020 7607 3629

e-mail: info@oberonbooks.com

www.oberonbooks.com

A catalogue record for this book is available from the British Library.

ISBN: 978-1-84002-836-2

Cover illustration by Frozen River

Printed in Great Britain by Antony Rowe Ltd, Chippenham.

Characters

CHRIS

JULIA

MARTIN

SARAH

This text is written to be performed bilingually.

Scenes with the same scene number are written to be performed simultaneously.

Within scenes:
Lines in bold are only signed and not spoken
<u>Lines underlined are only spoken and not signed</u>
<u>**Lines underlined and in bold are spoken and signed**</u>
Lines without additional formatting can be signed and/or spoken

here lies the heart of the difference between grief
as we imagine it and grief as it is…the unending
absence that follows, the void, the very
opposite of meaning, the relentless succession
of moments during which we will confront the
experience of meaninglessness itself
Joan Didion

Keep on playing our favourite song
Turn it up while you're gone
It's all I've got
When you're in my head
And you're in my head
So I need it
Queens of the Stone Age

Music coming through static.

1

An expectant silence.

CHRIS	**How do you get –**
JULIA	How do you get –
CHRIS	**From Johnny Cash**
JULIA	(Who's Johnny Cash?)
MARTIN	(Did she just say who's Johnny Cash?)
CHRIS	**He's a legend.**
JULIA	Okay from Johnny Cash to – ?
MARTIN	Nine Inch Nails!
SARAH	The Clash! Easy easy!
CHRIS	**No and no.**
JULIA	(Why isn't it ever music I know?)
MARTIN	(How can you not know Johnny Cash?)
JULIA	It's just music –
MARTIN	Ah but music isn't just music –
ALL	Music is also everything else!
CHRIS	**Johnny Cash to Hall and Oates.**
SARAH	To *Hall and Oates?*
MARTIN	You're taking the piss.
JULIA	This is like Mornington Crescent.
CHRIS	**And in one move.**
MARTIN	In one move? Fuck!

JULIA	Did Hall & Oates do 'Solid as a Rock'?
MARTIN	No, dear.
SARAH	Hall & Oates are white soul, Julia. You know, (*She attempts a little dance.*) blue-eyed soul.
MARTIN & CHRIS	(*Ad lib.*) No! Don't dance!
SARAH	You're so mean to me. I'm a great dancer.
MARTIN	You look ill.
CHRIS	**He's right, baby.**
SARAH	Hall & Oates don't connect with anything. That's the whole thing about Hall & Oates.
CHRIS	**Is that your final answer?**
MARTIN	No, hold on, work backwards. Were they in another band before they went solo?
CHRIS	**It won't help you.**
MARTIN	Who produced them? Who discovered them? What label were they on?
JULIA	Is it about facial hair?
MARTIN	Julia! I believe it's beer time! (*She hits him, but she goes anyway.*)
JULIA	Cheeky bugger.
MARTIN	And get one for yourself, darlin'.
CHRIS	**I'll have to hurry you.**
MARTIN	Okay. Okay. Bluff.
SARAH	Yes, bluff. There's no connection.
CHRIS	**Final answer?**

SARAH & MARTIN	Final answer.
CHRIS	**I got three words for you losers. De La Soul.**
SARAH	Oh…
MARTIN	*Three Feet High and Rising*?
SARAH	Samples. How were possibly supposed to get that?
MARTIN	Julia? Where's that beer?
CHRIS	**Never call bluff.**
SARAH	I love you. You freak.
CHRIS	**There's always a connection.**
SARAH	I love you.
MARTIN	And a sick bucket while you're out there, Julia.
CHRIS	**Everything's connected.**

'Tunic (Song for Karen)' by Sonic Youth. Torrid music.

2

SARAH stands holding the phone.
She has just heard terrible, terrible news.
She is shaking her head.
MARTIN tries to catch her eye.
He looks at her questioningly.

3

SARAH is sitting, dazed, gazing unseeing.
MARTIN sits helplessly, a useless hand on her shoulder.
He doesn't know what to do.

CHRIS sits in another chair watching them both.

4

SARAH and MARTIN are sitting apart.
SARAH is red-eyed.
MARTIN smiles at her.
SARAH's head sinks and she cries again.
SARAH is crying, shaking her head slowly.

SARAH   Oh no oh no oh no oh no oh no oh no oh no

MARTIN can do nothing.
CHRIS is not there.
The music continues.

5

A gig. Never.

CHRIS   Anticipation could not have been higher at the G-Mex Centre for the long-awaited return of Manchester's own. It's been twenty years and maybe the quiff's a little thinner, eyes a little baggier, the bellies a wee bit broader, but they walk out onto the stage like cocky teenagers. And the only singer that ever mattered leans into the microphone to utter the words: 'Oh Manchester, where have I been all your life?' and the music shimmers into our hearts again. Over the top of Joyce and Rourke's supple rhythm section, Johnny's guitar still sparkles and swoons, and Morrissey is, as he always was, Britain's single greatest front man. Truculent? Devious? Unreliable? We wouldn't want him any other way. Throw your homework onto the fire: it's 2007 and The Smiths are back to save us all.

6

JULIA	headache he said
SARAH	So you thought
JULIA	got him an Aspirin and we
SARAH	what he just
JULIA	moment we were talking, the next
SARAH	(*Cries.*)
JULIA	It's too
SARAH	I can't
JULIA	My little brother
SARAH	Please tell me he
JULIA	He didn't, it
SARAH	He's gone he's gone he's gone

6a

CHRIS	**I was at my sister's.**
	She had cooked.
	I was complaining of a headache.
	We were talking.
	And then
	Suddenly
	She's stood up, with her mouth open.
	I think she must be screaming.
	Maybe I'm on the floor.
	I don't know.
	Where am I?

7

MARTIN	Brain haemorrhage?
SARAH	That's what
MARTIN	Fuck. The poor
SARAH	He went into a coma and
MARTIN	So life support or
SARAH	But the doctors said he would never
MARTIN	No what they
SARAH	She didn't even call me
MARTIN	Oh God, Sarah
SARAH	(*Cries.*)
MARTIN	Oh God, Sarah, I'm sorry.

7a

CHRIS **Now I'm in an ambulance.**
Now I'm above an ambulance.
Now I'm above the trees.
Now I'm breathing night air.
Now I'm above the sky.
Now I'm remembering a song.
**I can see for miles and miles and miles and
miles and miles.**

8

SARAH	Did you hear that?
JULIA	Hear what?

SARAH   …

That.

JULIA   I don't hear anything.

SARAH   You can't hear it?

8a

CHRIS   …

…

Can you see me?

Can you hear me?

…

…

9

MARTIN and SARAH together.
They are crying with laughter.
Or are they crying?
They subside.
They look at each other.
This sets them off again.

9a

CHRIS half laughs along, the reflex of old friends.
But he stops.

10

SARAH has just stopped crying.

JULIA   We don't cry in our family. It's not our way.

SARAH   Chris was quite emotional with me.

JULIA   He'll have got that from our father.

SARAH   It's not a bad thing is it?

JULIA   Some girls they like a soft one. Means they can wrap him round their finger.

SARAH   Is that what happened with you?

JULIA   With me?

SARAH   Yes and your ex-husband

JULIA   Edward.

SARAH   Edward yes.

JULIA   Lasted six months then she gave him the push. Silly man. I feel sorry for him. Not that I'd have him back though. Not in a million years.

10a

MARTIN reads a music magazine. He is absorbed in an article. CHRIS stands behind watching him. CHRIS starts reading the article over MARTIN's shoulder. Almost as if sensing his presence, MARTIN starts crying. CHRIS is so absorbed in the article, it takes him a few moments to notice.

11

SARAH crying.
MARTIN consoling her.

MARTIN   I am so sorry, Sarah.

            You have to think of the good things.

            You have to I don't know honour that memory or else it's…

The things you shared

SARAH cries harder.

I wish there was something I could say.

You know if he were here he'd be saying, snap out of it, Sarah.

You have to start looking forward.

You can't do this to yourself, Sarah.

11a

CHRIS is very close to SARAH. Maybe head resting against her shoulder.

CHRIS
I am here and I am not here.

I am now and I am not now.

We are together and we are not together.

You don't have to listen to Martin

You don't have to snap out of it.

You don't have to look forward.

12

JULIA has an awkward arm round SARAH.

SARAH is crying, with abandonment.

JULIA sneaks a look at her watch.

13

SARAH
tell me I'm being fucking brave I'm not brave I'm scared and stupid and wrecked and crying and I've lost the only man I've ever loved and I'm scared Martin I'm scared because I'm all on my fucking own because he went and died on me just died on me without warning and

he fucking abandoned me to this grief this dog
that's eating my fucking heart out of my chest
I'm the one left here feeling this way and living
like this and being like this and I don't want to
live this life Martin I don't want to live this life

13a

JULIA alone. She looks upwards confidently.

JULIA   **Please God.**
Please God.
Don't let me cry.
I don't want to cry.

She searches upwards.

…

God?

14

Undertakers' brochures.

SARAH   I'm sorry. (*Cries.*)

JULIA   I know it's hard, Sarah. It's hard for me too.

SARAH   I know, I'm sorry. (*Cries.*)

JULIA   You have to pull yourself together.

SARAH   That's a hard wood, isn't it?

JULIA   There's a time for politics and a time for

SARAH   He'd have hated this.

JULIA   He would have told you to pull yourself
together.

SARAH   I wish I could be so calm like you. (*Cries.*)

JULIA   There's only so much misery people will take.

14a

MARTIN and CHRIS. Ten years ago.

CHRIS   **Funeral music?**

MARTIN   **You know the song 'To Live Is To Fly'.**

CHRIS   **Nice.**

MARTIN   **I want everyone to sing along.**

CHRIS   **Will they know it?**

MARTIN   **Make a CD. Send it with the funeral invitations.**

CHRIS   **You don't do funeral invitations.**

MARTIN   **Upload it to a website.**

CHRIS   **I'm not sure, legally, we can do that.**

MARTIN   **I want those fuckers singing.**

15

SARAH   it is again

MARTIN   next door

SARAH   nearer than that

MARTIN   honestly, I

SARAH   please, just look in the

MARTIN   Sarah, these are old houses and

SARAH   think I'm going out of my

MARTIN   okay okay, I'll look I'll

15a

CHRIS explores the room as if for the first time.

16

SARAH
I'm stuck, Chris.

When I go to bed my eyes ache.

My skin's dry deep down.

I'm underground and I'm going to die here.

Like I'm cold to the centre of me and I'll never be warm.

Like everywhere is dark and the sun won't rise.

Like my body's glass and my heart's a bone and every moment is a hammer and I long to be broken.

16a

JULIA
I'm stuck, God.

When I go to bed my eyes ache.

My skin's dry deep down.

I'm underground and I'm going to die here.

Like I'm cold to the centre of me and I'll never be warm.

Like everywhere is dark and the sun won't rise.

Like my body's glass and my heart's a bone and every moment is a hammer and I long to be broken.

17

Static. Light. Solemnity.

Out of the static comes the Agnus Dei from Mozart's Missa Brevis in G (K49). It fades in and out of the static. It is perhaps not wholly recognisable.

All but SARAH interpret it.

SARAH is in a pew.

It's the funeral.

18

In a car. JULIA is driving. SARAH in the passenger seat. MARTIN is in the back.

JULIA   I drive to the church.

SARAH   I get a taxi to the church.

JULIA   Yes, I drive to the church because I will not be defeated.

MARTIN   I get a lift to the church with my old mate Radio Dave and his girlfriend.

JULIA   You can never call yourself lucky in situations like this and actually I've always thought talk of luck was vaguely blasphemous, but there's no denying that Christopher's death could have been worse.

CHRIS   **I am driven to the church, in the back of Long Black Limousine. It's the first time my body has travelled in a car since 1996 and my accident.**

He occupies the fourth seat in the back. Music: 'I Can See For Miles' The Who.

MARTIN   Radio Dave has made a wicked compilation which is designed to turn our car journey into an emotional journey. Which is so Radio Dave.

37

SARAH   I ask the cabbie to turn the music up. It's one of my favourites. But I just want to fill my head with music.

MARTIN   Turn it up, Radio Dave!

JULIA   Because of course ten or so years ago, Christopher had his accident. He was in intensive care for a while and for six hours it was touch and go, so…

MARTIN   I was driving. It was ten years ago something like that.

CHRIS   **We'd been to see the Super Furry Animals in Cardiff and we were driving back through the night. I can't remember the gig now.**

MARTIN   Can't remember the headliners; The Super Furries blew them off the stage and out of memory.

CHRIS   **I remember getting into the car like it happened to someone else.**

MARTIN   We were driving through the night and it's bright moonlight. And we pass one of those white chalk men cut into the side of a hill. He has one hand above his head like he's saying hello. And Chris starts waving.

CHRIS   **Apparently I was quite drunk.**

MARTIN   And I'm trying to concentrate on the road and Chris is singing 'Fool on the Hill' and saying, wave at the man.

CHRIS   **I was waving at a chalk man, according to Martin.**

MARTIN   And this other car comes out of nowhere.

CHRIS	**And according to the driver of the other car, we came out of nowhere.**
JULIA	It was a Sunday morning and I had one of my heads so I'd gone back to bed. When I woke up Edward said there was a message on the machine.
SARAH	I'd only known Chris six months. We met at a Manic Street Preachers gig. Richey Edwards smashed up his guitar at the end of 'You Love Us' and Chris squeezed my hand and said sometimes only clichés will do. Martin called me. It was a Sunday.
JULIA	As if I couldn't have got up. A message from the hospital and he doesn't even lift the phone just carries on sitting there eating Pringles and watching *Eastenders* or I don't know what. Disgusting and I said so.
SARAH	I was ill and couldn't go to the gig which was lucky as it turned out though at the time
MARTIN	Sat in the hospital all night waiting for Chris to wake up feeling like a
JULIA	Martin didn't leave a number and they didn't have Caller ID so I had to ring round all the
MARTIN	Holding Chris's hand and singing his favourite songs
SARAH	I got a train and found the ward and there was Martin, singing
MARTIN	'Don't blame it on the sunshine, don't blame it on the moonlight, don't blame it on the good times, blame it on the boogie'.
JULIA	Martin there without a scratch on him

SARAH	Martin's covered in bruises and the leg of his jeans has been cut away and
JULIA	And I lean over him and kiss my brother's forehead and
SARAH	And there's a strange woman
JULIA	And there's a strange woman by his bed.
MARTIN	And at 7.00 that evening, he wakes up.
SARAH	He opens his eyes.
JULIA	And at 7.13 he opens his eyes and he looks around and he smiles at me.
SARAH	And he looks at me and says:
CHRIS	**Hey baby. Will you marry me?**
SARAH	And without thinking I say, yes, yes I'll marry you.
CHRIS	**My voice sounds strange in my head.**
JULIA	Rehearse the worst then you are always prepared. Get your crying done inwardly. I'm not one for letting it all hang out. Tears are a shame to oneself and a burden to others.
CHRIS	**I can't drive anyway but I don't get into a car again.**
MARTIN	I have to drive for work but every route drives through that night.
SARAH	Chris won't even get in a car on our wedding day. Horse and cart, I kid you not.
JULIA	I am a back-on-the-horse person because otherwise you're just a victim of events aren't you? So I drive, of course I drive, even to the church I drive.

19

A gig. Never.

CHRIS   The Beatles haven't played live in the UK
for over a year and the long gap since the
last album led some to expect the worst. But
tonight, at the Albert Hall, the new world tour
kicked off with a full unveiling of a brand new
album. The first thing to report is the band's
new stage outfits. Bright military-style knee-
length jackets in very *un*military green, blue,
red and yellow satin are a marked difference
from the dark grey stage suits of only a couple
of years ago. The Albert Hall would hardly be
most people's choice to launch a world tour, but
today if anything it complemented the pastiche
Victoriana of the band's new look. But the music
was the star. Even those of us who are used to
these boys' miraculous way with a melody were
stunned by the diversity and sheer audacity of
the tunes that swarmed from the stage, from
the brass-enhanced stomp-a-long opener, right
through to its sinuously epic finale, performed
with the assistance of a concert orchestra. Last
night, the boys from Liverpool transformed
this unpromising corner of west London into a
psychedelic fairground and no one at the Hall
could disagree that 1967 will be the year of
Sgt Pepper.

20

CHRIS signs MARTIN's words only.

SARAH   What are you doing?

MARTIN   Looking through your record collection.

SARAH   Oh be my guest.

MARTIN   And I'm afraid I have some rather bad news.

SARAH   What?

MARTIN   You'd better sit down.

SARAH   Why? What's happened?

MARTIN   Someone's broken into your house and (*Deep breath.*) they've left the first Spiritualized album in your collection.

SARAH   Oh ha ha.

MARTIN   ASBO the lot of them, I say.

SARAH   It's mine, as well you know.

MARTIN   I see. An unwanted gift.

SARAH   I like Spritualized.

MARTIN   Sh now. It's the grief talking.

SARAH   …

MARTIN   What?

          CHRIS withdraws, stops signing. He will enter JULIA's orbit, briefly.

SARAH   Nothing. I – it's okay.

MARTIN   (*Looks behind him.*) What?

SARAH   Nothing.

21

JULIA is washing up.
She breaks a glass.
She tries not to cry.
She manages.
She disposes of the glass carefully.

22

SARAH   Are you alright in there Julia?

JULIA   Just a glass.

              To avoiding being heard they use gestures, mouthing and SSE.

MARTIN   **How's it been with** (*Points towards JULIA.*)**?**

SARAH   (*Rolls eyes.*)

MARTIN   **I presume Mozart was her idea.**

SARAH   **You think I'd have chosen Agnus Dei?**

MARTIN   **It wasn't even the Rufus Wainwright version.**

SARAH   **He's done a version?**

MARTIN   ***Has*** **he? I'll tape it for you.**

SARAH   **Tape? What is this, the seventies?**

MARTIN   **She was watching me in church, you know. Like she was cross I was there or something.**

SARAH   **You know what she's like. She thinks being principal mourner is like winning a medal.**

MARTIN   **I didn't realise they were so close. They're so different.**

SARAH   **After the accident, when Chris's hearing started to go, she was the one who taught him Sign.**

MARTIN   **She taught him?**

SARAH   **Yes. Did a night class, then would come and teach him what she'd learned.**

MARTIN   **Like having a secret language.**

SARAH   **You know she wants me out?**

MARTIN   **What, out of here?**

SARAH   **That's what she implied.**

MARTIN   **You're kidding me**.

23

JULIA   I'm sure we can resolve this equitably.

SARAH   I said: I'm still in shock.

JULIA   Of course, of course.

SARAH   I mean, it's hard for me, for you it must be

JULIA   Christopher was my brother. I'll never get over it.

SARAH   (*Cries.*) I'm sorry.

JULIA   Now is not the time, obviously.

SARAH   You've been so

JULIA   Not at

SARAH   No you have. We could never have bought anywhere so it

JULIA   At the time his need was greater than

SARAH   He carried me over the threshold. Silly but

JULIA   Of course it does leave us with a situation.

SARAH   I understand.

JULIA   But as I say, I'm sure we can resolve this equitably.

24

MARTIN	**Cow**.
SARAH	**We've got to talk about it at some point**.
MARTIN	**Yeah but his body still *warm***.
SARAH	…
MARTIN	Shit, I'm sorry.
SARAH	I'm okay, really, I'm okay.
MARTIN	You look like shit.
SARAH	Once again. Thank you.
MARTIN	You're entitled to look like shit.
SARAH	I'm like a song. I want someone who'll watch over me.
MARTIN	You know I'm around if you need me.
SARAH	I know that. Thank you, Martin.
MARTIN	You know what you need?
SARAH	What?
MARTIN	Some Dylan.
SARAH	Some what?
MARTIN	Early stuff. *Blonde on Blonde*, something like that.
SARAH	I don't know…
MARTIN	It's full of life. It'll cheer you up.
SARAH	It's my husband's funeral, Martin, not a bad day at the office.
MARTIN	Trust me on this.

Goes to the stereo.

SARAH   You think everything can be solved by music don't you Martin.

MARTIN   (*Thinks about it.*) Um.
Yes. Yes I do.

SARAH   Unbelievable.

MARTIN   (*Taking out the record.*) There's an exuberance that Dylan brought to this period of his life, which I think you'll find very hey hey hey I thought you said you didn't do tapes?

SARAH   What do you mean?

MARTIN   My lord, I present exhibit A. (*Holds up a tape.*)

SARAH   What is it?

MARTIN   It's got your name on it.

SARAH   It's not mine.

MARTIN   Is that not your writing?

SARAH   No, I think

MARTIN   Catch.

SARAH   I think it's

MARTIN   Your attention please, this is your pilot speaking, please fasten your seat belts and return your trays to the upright position, we are ready to party.

Puts the needle on the record. Bob Dylan's 'I Want You'. SARAH stares at the tape in her hands.

25

A gig. Never.

CHRIS   Last night at the Alhambra, Bob Dylan delighted
         a packed and enthusiastic crowd by playing a
         selection of his greatest songs exactly like they
         sound on the record. Longtime Zimmermaniacs
         were delighted by his ninety-minute request-
         fuelled encore, especially when the sprightly
         folk-rock legend crowd-surfed during 'Like a
         Rolling Stone'.

26

SARAH alone.

From some old drawer she has produced a cheap plastic Walkman.

She takes a deep breath and picks up the compilation.

She stares at her name on the cover.

She wells up.

She looks up, fighting to control it.

Back to the tape.

She takes the tape out and places it down.

She removes the inlay card and scrutinises it carefully.

There's nothing on it but her name.

She picks up the tape and examines it, front and back.

Nothing.

She notices that the tape is slightly loose round the spindles.

She goes to her bag and finds a biro.

She puts the biro in one of the spindles and winds the tape carefully so that it is taut.

She examines the Walkman.

She opens the Walkman.

She hasn't used it for some time so is unsure which way the tape goes.

She works it out.

She puts the headphones on.

She presses play and closes her eyes.

After a few seconds she realises nothing is happening.

She opens her eyes.

She presses stop.

She stares at the Walkman.

She presses eject and takes out the tape.

She puts it back in and presses play again.

Nothing.

She opens the battery compartment.

It's empty.

She rummages in the drawer.

She reaches for the TV remote, takes those batteries out and places them in the Walkman.

She adjusts the headphones and presses play.

Four seconds hiss.

Song begins.

It is Micah P Hinson & The Gospel of Progress singing 'I Still Remember'.

She listens, not sure what she is listening for.

JULIA, MARTIN and CHRIS interpret the song.

She listens for 30 seconds and speeds forward.

We surface in the middle of 'First Time I Saw You' (demo version) by Euros Childs.

She listens, not sure what she is listening for.

JULIA, MARTIN and CHRIS interpret the song.

20 seconds then she speeds forward.

'I Can't Explain' [Live at Leeds] by The Who.

She recognises it after ten seconds or so and rolls her eyes.

What is she listening for?

She does not know.

She listens.

27

JULIA walks around her house removing pictures of CHRIS from photo frames, from off the fridge, anywhere they might surprise her.

28

SARAH is still listening.
Fast Forward
The Beatles 'Because'
Fast Forward
De La Soul 'Eye Know'
Fast Forward
Pavement 'From Now On'
Fast Forward

29

JULIA, kneeling, spreads out on the floor the photographs of CHRIS.

30

MARTIN's den.

MARTIN	Yes you have, you came for dinner.
SARAH	But we didn't see in here.
MARTIN	Chris did but
SARAH	Ah. It's a guy space, I understand.
MARTIN	Not a guy space exactly

SARAH   It smells like a guy space.

MARTIN   Where no woman has been before.

SARAH   I feel privileged.

MARTIN   Virgin territory.

SARAH   Lucky me.

MARTIN   You're penetrating the inner sanctum.

SARAH   Okay, that metaphor ends right now.

MARTIN   Fair enough. So, to what do I owe the honour, etc.

SARAH   What are the rules for making a compilation tape?

MARTIN   The rules?

SARAH   Yeah, the guy rules. The rules that govern the making of compilation tapes that all guys seem to know.

MARTIN   Well, I could tell you, but then I'd have to kill you.

SARAH   If you don't tell me, I'll kill *you.*

MARTIN   Well, some ground rules. A compilation tape is a two-act drama. First half – open with something fast, striking, upbeat, grab their attention. Then once you've got it, you can explore your softer side, some acoustic numbers, a little folk maybe, building to a strong first half closer. Second side, open with something experimental, a little difficult, this is the place for your Captain Beefheart, your Can; then you repeat the formula of side one but build to something epic, anthemic but complex, before ending off on something smaller and lighter. A novelty song, a tv theme tune, something like that.

SARAH   Okay. And does the compilation tape have to
               have a theme?

MARTIN   You have your basic cheer-up tape (hope you're
               enjoying that by the way), there's your seduction
               tape, naturally, a dance mix – not for the
               choreographically challenged (sorry Sarah) –

               She hits him.

               and some standard varieties, the A-Z tape, the
               songs-with-cities-animals-or-names-in-the-title
               tape, that sort of thing, but normally eclectic is
               the way to go.

SARAH   If you were given a compilation tape, say, and it
               was pretty random, but it had two songs by the
               same artist –

MARTIN   (*Sharp intake of breath.*)

SARAH   What?

MARTIN   Rookie error.

SARAH   Is it?

MARTIN   The genius of the compilation tape lies in the
               spread of music and the blankness of the format.
               If you don't like the first one, maybe you'll like
               the second. It's got to look casual. Two songs
               by the same artist means one of two things:
               either you are desperate to make the recipient
               agree with your taste (very uncool) or – worse
               still – (*Swallows hard.*) you don't actually know
               very much music.

SARAH   This tape has two Smiths songs on it. *And*
               something by Morrissey.

MARTIN   Shut *up!* Who made it?

SARAH	...
	Chris.
	I think Chris was making it for me before he
MARTIN	Okay. That's weird.
SARAH	It is, isn't it?
MARTIN	Or not. Maybe he was halfway through redoing it.
SARAH	Perhaps. Look, I don't know all the songs. Is it okay if I have a look at your records?
MARTIN	Be my guest. Sure.

31

JULIA is hesitant. She wants to offer the photographs to a God but she feels self-conscious.

32

MARTIN	You okay there?
SARAH	Mm fine.
MARTIN	Just give us a shout if
SARAH	I will.

33

JULIA waits with the photographs spread out on the floor.
She expects something to happen. Something magical.
It doesn't.
Of course it doesn't.

34

SARAH looking through records. Occasionally she takes one out and examines it. Sometimes she writes something down.

Silence.

MARTIN sighs.

SARAH Something the matter?

MARTIN No, no. You –

Silence.

MARTIN sighs.

SARAH What?

MARTIN It makes me nervous, that's all, looking through my music collection. It's like you're rifling through my unconscious.

SARAH You've nothing to be ashamed of.

MARTIN I know but

SARAH I promise I won't tell anyone about the fourth Oasis album.

MARTIN Actually that's a much-underrated

SARAH I'm joking.

MARTIN No but that's exactly what I

SARAH Honestly, stop panicking.

MARTIN Sorry.

Silence.

SARAH Is this the new Manics album?

MARTIN About a year old.

SARAH We used to love them.

MARTIN   I know.

SARAH   We met at a Manics gig.

MARTIN   I know.

SARAH   Richey smashed up his guitar and Chris
            squeezed my hand and said

MARTIN   Sometimes only a cliché will do, I know.

SARAH   Oh you know.

MARTIN   Yes. Though actually

SARAH   What?

MARTIN   Nothing.

            Silence.

SARAH   Why a tape?

MARTIN   How do you mean?

SARAH   Why wouldn't he just burn a CD? It's so much
            easier.

MARTIN   Burning a CD. It's so cold. Digital music means
            nothing. Analogue's the future, baby.

SARAH   What, you don't have an iPod?

MARTIN   (*Makes sign of the cross.*) Ah! The evil one!

SARAH   What, iPod?

MARTIN   (*Flinches.*)

SARAH   This is some audiophile snobbery thing isn't it.

MARTIN   The compression algorithms even on MP4 are –

SARAH   You're boring me already.

MARTIN   Just spreading the wisdom.

SARAH	(*Draws a horizontal line in the air.*) Autistic spectrum. (*Points to the right of the line.*) You.
MARTIN	It's been said before and I dare say
SARAH	(*Brandishing tape.*) Why did he make this for me?
MARTIN	Why does any man make a woman a tape?
SARAH	Oh here we go.
MARTIN	Though obviously in your case, he'd already –
SARAH	Yes, thank you.
MARTIN	Doesn't he usually make you tapes?
SARAH	He hasn't for a while. Not since his hearing went. So, I guess six years.
MARTIN	Which is just about pre-iPod anyway.
SARAH	I guess. … …
MARTIN	What is it?
SARAH	I think it means something.
MARTIN	Yeah: 'here's 25 songs you might like'.
SARAH	There's something odd. I can't put my finger on it but the tape doesn't make sense somehow. I need to listen to it again.
MARTIN	Okay.
SARAH	… You know I sometimes I feel he's there.
MARTIN	Like a phantom limb.

SARAH   Yeah, I guess.

        Corner of my eye, like he's just standing there.

MARTIN But he's not.

SARAH   No. He's not.

MARTIN Glad we got that one sorted out.

SARAH   Thanks. (*Going.*) By the way, Martin.

MARTIN Yeah?

SARAH   For a straight man, you have an awful lot of
        Girls Aloud.

MARTIN Hey, the production work on those albums is

        But she is gone.

35

A gig. Never.

CHRIS   It's hard to believe that it's been twenty years
        and that Nirvana have graduated to become
        elder statesmen of American rock. Not that
        they show any signs of slowing down. Their
        latest album, *Basra,* showed an unusually
        direct political edge after the return to themes
        of personal alienation and self-hatred that
        dominated their controversial double album,
        Bleeder in 2004. A great gig is always a revelation
        and those critics who felt that the album's
        politics was at the expense of great songs should
        think again. A storming Saturday night set at this
        year's Glastonbury Festival was dominated by
        the new album and every song emerged bright
        and clean, with just enough anthemic quality
        to unite the crowd but still with the sense of
        personal intensity and authenticity that we have
        come to expect from Kurt Cobain who was

visibly moved by the crowd's response – not least when they sang 'Happy Birthday' to his daughter Frances Bean who turns sixteen next month.

36

Phone.

JULIA   **I saw him in church**.

SARAH   …

Who?

JULIA   **Your friend. Martin. Not singing. Not even pretending to pray**.

SARAH   Well Martin's not religious.

JULIA   **Christopher would have.**

SARAH   Well, Julia, really, I don't know about

JULIA   **You didn't know everything about him. He talked to me. You didn't even learn his language properly**.

SARAH   Listen to me, Chris and I spoke very

JULIA   **He had belief. He had faith. He forgave Martin. Forgiveness comes from God.**

SARAH   It wasn't Martin's fault. Really Julia, you mustn't

JULIA   **Christopher loved his music. It was his world. What's worse than that.**

SARAH   A lot of things, this is ancient history.

JULIA   **He's my brother and my friend and I want I want I want him back**.

37

SARAH puts on the headphones.
She presses play and settles back.
JULIA, CHRIS and MARTIN interpret the song.
The Rakes 'We Danced Together'
SARAH listens.
She speeds forward.
The Raindrops 'Even Though You Can't Dance'
She speeds forward.
The Louvin Brothers 'I Wonder If You Know'
She speeds forward but stops, puzzled.
She presses play again.
The Louvin Brothers 'I Wonder If You Know'.
She gets out her mobile
Dials a number.
MARTIN answers.

SARAH It's country music.

MARTIN Hello. Who is this please?

SARAH The fourth song on side two. It's country music.

MARTIN All our operators are busy on other calls, please hold.

SARAH Chris hated country music.

MARTIN I know. I once blacked his eye for disrespecting Loretta Lynn.

SARAH So why's he putting a country song on this tape?

MARTIN I don't know. Is it cross-over? He liked The Jayhawks.

SARAH Listen.

She holds a Walkman headphone up to the phone and presses play.

MARTIN   Ouch. The Louvin Brothers. Hardcore.

SARAH   I don't get it. Why would he put music he doesn't like on a tape?

MARTIN   Maybe he thought *you* would like it.

Maybe it has personal significance for him.

Maybe he changed his mind. Maybe he put it on as a joke.

Maybe, maybe you should get some sleep.

SARAH   What time is it?

MARTIN   Two in the morning.

SARAH   Is it? Shit. I'm sorry.

MARTIN   Not at all. Any time. But obviously you know that.

SARAH   Night.

SARAH puts the headphones back on.
She hits fast forward and then play.
Damien Jurado 'I Am Still Here'
Interpreters back to work.
SARAH listens.

38

JULIA   **Please God**
Please God
I would swim through oceans of my tears
I would run from the edge of the earth
I would reach to the depths of my heart
I would bear all the pain in the air

For another minute with you.

39

SARAH presses fast forward.
The Smiths 'Ask'
SARAH presses fast forward.
Monkey Swallows the Universe 'MARTIN'
SARAH presses fast forward.
Dying strains of the song.
Static
Static
Static

SARAH   (*To herself.*) Chris…

Static
Static
Static
Did she hear something?
She takes off the headphones.
Static quieter.
She listens to the empty room.

SARAH   Chris?

She puts the headphones back on.
Static
Static

(*Internal.*) Chris.

JULIA   **God, please God, please God.**
         Where are you?

SARAH rewinds the tape and plays.
Static

Static
She stiffens.

SARAH   Oh God, Chris?

JULIA   **Don't leave me, not now**.

SARAH   What is this tape?
         What are you saying to me?
         / Reach out, Chris.
         Are you there?

JULIA   **God, hold my hand.**
         Walk beside me.

         SARAH lifts headphones away from her ears.
         Listens to the room.

SARAH   / You know this isn't like me.
         You know I'm not the type of person who
         believes in all this
         Please Chris
         Please please please
         Are you in here? Are you watching me?

JULIA   **Why won't you answer me?**
         What have I done to deserve this?
         Please God.
         For once in my life let me get what I want.
         I don't want another evening in an empty
         room.

SARAH   / If you're there
         Please be there
         I swear I will do anything
         I would pull up the roots of the earth
         I would pluck the stars from the sky
         For another minute with you

Answer me, fuck you
If you're here
Somewhere in the air around me
Just say
I'm here
That's all
I'm here

JULIA **If you're there**
Please be there
I swear I will do anything
I would pull up the roots of the earth
I would pluck the stars from the sky
For another minute with you
Answer me, fuck you
If you're here
Somewhere in the air around me
Just say
I'm here
That's all
I'm here

CHRIS **I'm here**
I'm here
I'm here

JULIA **/ You're dead to me.**
I'm dead to you.
We're dead, you and I.

SARAH Chris?
Oh God, yes.
I heard you.
<u>**You're here.**</u>

You're here.

SARAH cries.

JULIA stares up into nothing.

40

A gig. Never.

CHRIS   The sun has long fallen but the sunburned
             crowd in Philadelphia are still here, waiting
             for something, something. Haven't they had
             enough? Madonna, The Beach Boys, Dylan,
             Zeppelin. But the anticipation is like static in the
             crowd, you can feel it. Surging hope crackling
             through the 100,000 spectators. And now it
             comes. The lights dim, the crowd flick on their
             lighters. We hear Dick Clark announcing the
             biggest surprise of this incredible day. Only Live
             Aid could have coaxed this man out of a decade
             of retirement. The strains of Richard Strauss's
             'Also Sprach Zarathustra' ring out across the JFK
             Stadium. The curtain snatches aside impatiently.
             And he's here. 100,000 screams issue from
             100,000 American throats. Hair jet black, slim-
             hipped, all in black leather, that cocky half-smile
             projected across the massive screens flanking the
             stage. It's him, it's him. Will he feed the world?
             Who knows. Will he ever perform again? Who
             can say. But at midnight in America, on 13
             July 1986, let it be written: Elvis is back in the
             building.

41

MARTIN has a plastic bag of old tapes.

The English is very emotional. The Sign – performed by
JULIA and CHRIS – is flat.

MARTIN	This is crazy
SARAH	go on say what you
MARTIN	look I'm worried about
SARAH	have to worry about me I'm fine I'm
MARTIN	well I do, okay
SARAH	sure but actually I don't care what
MARTIN	This isn't like you
SARAH	I know what I'm doing
MARTIN	Do you? Actually?
SARAH	Martin I heard him.
MARTIN	Oh Sarah come on
SARAH	I heard him. I was listening to that tape to the end of that tape and the song ends and there's no more music just a couple of minutes of blank tape and I'm listening and I hear something in the static in the blankness of the tape and I really concentrate really hard and suddenly just a flash just for a second I hear his voice.
MARTIN	Sarah you don't do this, you hate this kind of
SARAH	I don't want to have a fucking debate about
MARTIN	I'm not trying to have
SARAH	Are you going to help me or
MARTIN	course I'm going to
SARAH	Because if you're not, you can fuck off.
MARTIN	Sarah, look at me, it's Martin, remember?
SARAH	Have you got the tapes?

MARTIN   … Yeah. These are old ones I don't need. Some
              might be blank. I'm not sure.

SARAH   And the tape recorder.

MARTIN   Yes.

SARAH   Has it got a good microphone?

MARTIN   I don't know, Sarah. I've never tried picking up
              the spirit world on it.

SARAH   You don't need to be like that.

MARTIN   Oh it's *me* being weird –

SARAH   People make recording of empty rooms,
              supposedly empty rooms, and they hear voices
              it's well-known –

MARTIN   It's well-known bullshit –

SARAH   What if he's here, Martin? What if he's standing
              right here? Listening to what we're saying?
              What if there are, actually, spirits in this room.
              Hundreds of spirits, who knows, drifting through
              this room, how stupid would you look to them?

MARTIN   Chris is dead, Sarah. Chris is dead and you can't
              bring him back and I hate that you're trying
              because he was my friend too, Sarah, he was my
              friend too.

              Silence.

SARAH   Right.

MARTIN   Sarah, I'm just saying

SARAH   No it's fine.

MARTIN   Sarah –

SARAH   It probably is bullshit. You're probably right.
              This is probably a waste of time.

MARTIN   I didn't mean

SARAH   But *if* he's talking to me, Martin, whether all this
         is bullshit or not, just in case I'm wrong, I have
         to listen. I have to listen, Martin.

MARTIN   …

         Okay.

SARAH   And we'll see.

MARTIN   We will.

42

A gig. Never.

CHRIS   It's 1967 at the Madison Square Gardens and
         one thing is certain: the Kinks have just broken
         America.

43

*Queens of the Stone Age 'In My Head'. It should run
through until the beginning of Sc. 49.*

An empty room.

A tape recorder sits on a table.

*A plug-in microphone with a small stand is propped up
next to it, pointed out into the room.*

44

Phone call.

MARTIN   Julia?

JULIA   **That's right.**

MARTIN   It's Martin.

Chris's friend.

From school.

JULIA   **Oh yes. Martin.**

MARTIN   I'm worried about Sarah.

JULIA   **You're what?**

MARTIN   Julia. I can barely hear you. Your music's very loud.

JULIA   **Is it?**

MARTIN   I'd like to talk about Sarah.

JULIA   **What about her?**

MARTIN   I think she needs someone who'll watch over her.

45

An empty room.

A tape recorder sits on a table.

A plug-in microphone with a small stand is propped up next to it, pointed out into the room.

After a moment, MARTIN enters, quietly.

He sneaks slowly and carefully up to the microphone, making no sound.

He leans into the microphone.

MARTIN   Wooooooooooh.

He sneaks out again.

46

JULIA   **I'm going to rip you from my heart God.**
I am going to turn away from you.

Maybe I can't stop believing.

But I'm going to ignore you.

That's for not being there when I needed you.

That's for forty years of prayers and not so much as a howdyado

See how *you* like it, God.

47

SARAH is listening to the Walkman.

Martin is watching her.

They're both drinking tea.

Long wait.

Then Sarah screams, throwing her tea.

Martin collapses with laughter.

SARAH   You bastard.

MARTIN   Got you.

SARAH   You fucking bastard.

She cries.

MARTIN   Oh God, Sarah. It was a joke.

I just thought you'd

It was a joke

48

An empty room.

A tape recorder sits on a table.

A plug-in microphone with a small stand is propped up next to it, pointed out into the room.

CHRIS stands next to the microphone, signing directly into it.

CHRIS

I would pull up the roots of the earth
I would pluck the stars from the sky
I would swim through oceans of my tears
I would ride a thousand wild horses
I would revisit the battlefields
I would balance on the top of the world
I would run from the edge of the earth
I would reach to the depths of my heart
I would walk among sunspots
I would crawl through my worst memories
I would sail through nightmares
I would walk ten thousand miles in the
mouth of a graveyard
I would exhume the mass graves
I would eat iron and drink barbed wire
For another minute with you.

49

MARTIN   She's taking it really badly.

JULIA   Can one take such a thing well?

MARTIN   Well you know what I mean.

JULIA   I'm not heartless I didn't expect her to leave
            tomorrow

MARTIN   She's not in a state to start looking for
            somewhere to live

JULIA   A month's notice is the customary

MARTIN   They lived together in that place for how long:
            seven years?

JULIA   Oh well if we're talking about legal rights / I
            have legal rights too

MARTIN   No no, really I – Julia, I seem to keep saying the wrong thing.

JULIA   Is there a right thing?

MARTIN   Words don't

JULIA   No they

MARTIN   always come out

JULIA   Better to just

MARTIN   Yes yes.

JULIA   You did that magazine with Christopher, didn't you?

MARTIN   Oh you mean at school? Yes.

JULIA   I still have a copy somewhere.

MARTIN   Really? Wow, more than I do.

JULIA   It'll be in a box somewhere.

MARTIN   Our slogan was: music isn't just music, music is also everything else.

JULIA   When Christopher was eight, most people our age wanted Rubik's cubes or whatever. He wanted a tape recorder.

MARTIN   Oh. Right.

JULIA   Mum and dad got him one with two tapes. He would record the Top 40. Then he would listen to them, and write little reviews in his notebook. Then he would re-record the show, removing the DJ and adding his own links between the songs. He was very good actually; we would listen to them in the car.

MARTIN   That terrible thing: the birth of a music journalist.

JULIA   There are parts of the South Downs that I still can't see without thinking of Christopher.

MARTIN   No yes of course.

JULIA   It drove dad crazy because we weren't allowed to talk when Christopher's tapes were playing, so there were terrific rows.

MARTIN   Are those tapes in a box somewhere?

JULIA   Lord no.

MARTIN   That's a shame because

JULIA   So when he lost his hearing after your accident, I believe it ripped the heart out of him. Not able to hear the music he loved

MARTIN   I don't think so, Julia. In fact he was very

JULIA   especially when you just walked away from

MARTIN   well hardly

JULIA   lived for his music and

MARTIN   was a serious blow but

JULIA   stone deaf after being so consumed by

MARTIN   really isn't right to describe

JULIA   never know what you can say nowadays

MARTIN   still enjoyed music though it was different of course

JULIA   felt like I lost him then so

MARTIN   once a music journalist, always a

JULIA   to lose all that

MARTIN   didn't he really didn't

JULIA   my brother my brother my brother

49a

CHRIS   The first record I bought was 'Our Lips Are Sealed' in Woolworths on the High Street in 1983. Top pop trivia fact: on the b-side of the single is a version of the same song in Urdu.

When I was eleven my parents bought me a tape player. I used to make my own pop radio shows and they used to play them in the car.

When I was a teenager, Martin and me did a fanzine at school. It was called *Wah* – I forget why. We reviewed records and wrote about gigs and talked about great how music was and how shit music was and how it really ought to save the world and how maybe it had and we just didn't know it and sometimes we invented bands that didn't exist but should and once, after an obnoxious David Bowie gig, we reviewed the gig it would have been in a perfect world.

We were obsessed with top five lists.

We dismissed people for being too rock.

We thought the NME Indie Charts were much too inclusive.

We said music wasn't just music: music was also everything else.

We couldn't have been happier.

The last record I bought I bought online the afternoon before I died. *The Avalanche* by Sufjan Stevens. His songs have the best titles.

50

A gig. Never.

CHRIS   The Grammys have seen many great performers
but the 2003 ceremony was something else.
After accepting his lifetime achievement award,
Otis Redding began what was scheduled as
a five-minute closing medley of soul classics.
Well, we got that, but then he cut through the
applause to ask the audience of record industry
insiders and bigwigs, 'Do y'all wanna hear
some more?' And for a moment, even the
most jaded music executive, rock journo and
record promoter just became a fan again, as
Otis took us through a blistering ninety-minute
work out through his back catalogue, testing the
improvisational powers of the podium band to
the utmost, but bringing everyone to their feet
for the triumphant finale of 'A Change is Gonna
Come' a nod to fellow soul survivor Sam Cooke,
sat on the front row, tears of rapture streaming
down his face.

51

SARAH and JULIA sit, side by side.
The sound of an empty room is deafening.
They are listening to a recording of the room they are in,
at another time.
Both of them strain to hear CHRIS.
They could be praying.

CHRIS   **I can see for miles and miles**
I can see for miles and miles
I can see for miles and miles
and miles and miles and miles

JULIA glances at SARAH.

She squeezes SARAH's hand.

52

JULIA signs, except for CHRIS's one line, which CHRIS signs. Maybe sometimes CHRIS joins in the signing.

MARTIN   Okay Chris, news:

1. The Magnetic Fields album is a bit disappointing.

2. The Weird Folk thing never went anywhere. You owe me a tenner.

3. In fact that makes £65 you owe me. £40 for Reading and £15 because Lady Sovereign has sort of broken America.

4. I think it's safe to come out now: the Stereophonics have gone away.

5. The NME has done the impossible. Yes, it's even more shit than it was last year.

6. The site is getting 10,000 hits a day. I think we should accept contributions online what do you think? Do you want me to tell Sarah?

7. Come back. I miss you.

8. Richard Hawley's been nominated for a Brit award. I shit you not.

9. No I mean it. Come back. Joke's over.

10. I took a drive yesterday. I got an urge to get out of town. I thought I'd drive down to that club where we first saw Grandaddy, and Mogwai, and The Eels, and where you said that you thought Camera Obscura could go all the way. Which is a long drive, so I put one of our car tapes on. It was one you made ten years ago. And anyway, I'm listening to this tape and I'm saying stuff like 'Why the fuck d'you put this

on?' and 'Don't tell me you like this' and it's just
me in the car so I'm saying it out loud and we
pass, because we have to, the place, the place
where

and on the tape it's 'I Am Not Willing' by Moby
Grape, which I've always

and I kind of slow down sort of superstitiously
or it's maybe that
things slow down
and and

okay, because this is the weird thing

I'm driving and suddenly
you say
Turn it up, I love this one.
and I turn round to look at you

and I lose control of the car. And luckily there's
no one coming the other way and there's no one
behind me, in fact there's no one as far as the
eye can see

and I can see for miles and miles and miles

and the car's stopped sideways across the road
and I'm crying like a fucking idiot and I just
miss you so badly, my buddy, my comrade-in-
arms, my partner-in-crime, my mate, my music
brother, my pal, my old friend, my friend.

53

SARAH   Listen to this.

MARTIN   Is this a wind up?

SARAH   It's very faint but it's there.

MARTIN   Don't tell me. You've found Caspar the Friendly
            Ghost.

SARAH   Wait and see.

MARTIN   Right.

SARAH   Okay, you ready?

MARTIN   …

SARAH   Okay.

            SARAH sticks the tape in the machine.
            She turns the volume up.
            It's the sound of her front room.

SARAH   You have to listen hard.

            The sound builds. Then, in the background, very very
            faintly, so faint that maybe we're not even sure we can
            hear it, there's Aimee Mann's 'That's How I Knew This
            Story Would Break My Heart'.

            Can you hear that?

MARTIN   What am I supposed to be hearing?

SARAH   Music, listen.

            Perhaps cheat it a little more clearly, but still very much
            behind the white noise.

MARTIN   Oh yes.

SARAH   You can hear it right?

MARTIN   'That's How I Knew This Story Would Break
            My Heart'.

SARAH   Excuse me?

MARTIN   It's a song by Aimee Mann called 'That's How I
            Knew This Story Would Break My Heart'.

SARAH   I *knew* it was Aimee Mann. I *love* Aimee Mann.

MARTIN   Well whoop de do. And your point is?

SARAH   It wasn't playing when I recorded this. Not
                upstairs, not downstairs, not in the street, not
                next door. But now it's on the tape.

MARTIN   Right yes but

SARAH   Yes *and* here's the thing:
                that song is on the compilation.

MARTIN   Is it.

SARAH   Yes. The tape he made me, that song is on there.
                Somehow, somehow he's pushing that song
                through the ether to me.

MARTIN   Okay I

SARAH   You see?

                *MARTIN goes over and presses stop, then eject. He examines
                the tape.*

                It's just an ordinary tape.

MARTIN   Have you listened to the rest of this?

SARAH   Not yet.

MARTIN   You should.

SARAH   I will.

MARTIN   Because you'll find that in a couple of minutes,
                Chris will start pushing 'You Tore Me Down' by
                the Flaming Groovies through the ether.

SARAH   Right.
                What?

MARTIN   Next up on Afterlife FM will be 'Funky Gibbon'
                by The Goodies.

SARAH   Okay, what are you talking about?

MARTIN   It's an old mixtape of mine. You're just hearing
           what was on there before, bleeding through.

SARAH   How does that

MARTIN   This was a tape I was making for a girl at work.
           I started with Aimee Mann, show your feminine
           side, then some Beatlish pop-rock to ease her
           into guy music; then a bit of nostalgic fun with
           the Goodies. I think then I went trip-hop for
           some reason.

SARAH   Okay but
           Okay but still
           …
           …
           Oh bollocks.

MARTIN   If you're worried about taping over it, she ended
           up shagging an A&R man at Sanctuary, so –
           You weren't worried about that, were you.

SARAH   I feel like a total fucking idiot.

MARTIN   If it helps, I feel like you're a total fucking idiot
           as well.

SARAH   Thanks.
           At least I didn't put 'Funky Gibbon' on a
           seduction tape.

MARTIN   Deny its sexual allure if you dare.

SARAH   But still, I know he's
           there, he's

MARTIN   Sarah –

SARAH   (*Cries.*)

MARTIN   I know what you need.

SARAH   No Dylan!

MARTIN   Wine.

SARAH   I'm just so tired Martin.

MARTIN   I know. How do we live?

SARAH   You know when a song starts with all the
                instruments playing their stuff, but it feels loose
                and chaotic. There's a kind of rhythm but it feels
                casual somehow. And then the drums come
                in, and everything locks into place, everything
                makes sense. That's what he was in my life. He
                walked into my life and everything made sense.
                He was the moment when the drums come in.

MARTIN   Yeah.
                …
                Like the song.

SARAH   The what song?
                The Aimee Mann?

MARTIN   Yeah.

SARAH   Does it?

MARTIN   I'll put it on.

SARAH   Where's my encore, Martin?
                Where's my comeback tour?
                Where's my blazing rock finale?

                Song starts.

MARTIN   Don't do air piano.

SARAH   Sorry.
                (Sorry.)
                …
                Love this:
                'anchor tattoo'!

(Sorry.)

They listen.

SARAH   (*0'46"*) What is this line?
            'Chanticleer'
            What's a chanticleer?

MARTIN   I don't know.

SARAH   (You're rubbish.)

            They listen. SARAH joins in on the title line. Not comically, not sentimentally. She just likes the song.

SARAH   (*1'42"*) That nearly spoils it for me.

MARTIN   What?

SARAH   Synthesiser strings. Eww.

MARTIN   Oh yeah.

            They listen.

MARTIN   Is it a good tape then?

SARAH   Chris's tape? Yeah. Yeah it is. Well. No, yeah it is. Sort of. Quite weird.

MARTIN   Weird how?

SARAH   It just doesn't hang together. It's so random.

MARTIN   Random is good. You should read Ian Macdonald's book about the Beatles. He talks about –

SARAH   Not listening, freakboy.

            They listen.

MARTIN   (*2'39"*) (*Mimes the drum intro.*)

SARAH   Oh so air drums is okay.

MARTIN   Air drums are a world away from air keyboards.

SARAH   (*Pulls face.*)

            They listen.

SARAH   …

            Why didn't I know it?

            Chris has all her albums. He never played me
            this.

MARTIN   This one's quite recent.

SARAH   Really?

MARTIN   2005, something like that.

SARAH   What?

MARTIN   What?

            SARAH takes the needle off the record.

SARAH   What did you say?

MARTIN   … I said this came out in 2005.

            Silence. SARAH's trying to figure something out.

SARAH   Chris's hearing totally went in 2002.

MARTIN   Yeah.

SARAH   This came out in 2005.

MARTIN   So?

SARAH   He couldn't possibly have heard this song.

MARTIN   Oh.

SARAH   Yeah.

MARTIN   Why do you put a song you've never heard on a
            mixtape?

SARAH   …

            Chris still bought records.

He liked the static cling when you first take a record out of an inner sleeve.

He liked labels and coloured vinyl and things cut into the run-out groove.

He liked lyric booklets and liner notes and gatefold sleeves.

He looked at song titles and imagined the songs.

MARTIN   Because music isn't just music. Music is also everything else.

SARAH   It's not the songs is it?

It's the titles.

I need your help, nerd boy.

54

JULIA speaks and uses SSE. If this creates an awkward stiltedness to the speech so much the better.

JULIA   Four weeks after my brother died, I drive out to the South Downs.

The landscape reminds me of day trips and picnics

My brother is twelve

Maybe younger.

His voice on the car stereo.

Songs and landscape.

Four weeks after he died, I find a place to park off the main road

and I sit in the car gazing out at the hills.

And I stare at them.

And I stare at them.

And even when I feel tears coming, I stare at them.

You will not defeat me, I said.

And I stared at the Downs for most of the afternoon.

So, eventually, they lost their horror for me.

I burned this new memory of the Downs into my eyes and heart like pressing a key into plasticine.

I look at them quite often now.

They no longer – and I am glad of this – remind me of my brother

my brother my brother my brother

55

We're hearing Micah P Hinson and the Gospel of Progress 'I Still Remember'.

SARAH   Is this the only one we can't get?

MARTIN   There's the folky one on side two.

SARAH   We're guessing that as 'I Am Still Here', aren't we?

MARTIN   Oh yeah. So it's just this one.

                      They listen.

                      'With You Tonight'?
                      'You Fell Asleep'?

SARAH   Maybe.

                      They listen.

                      'I Still Remember'?

MARTIN   It's more title-y.

SARAH   (*Writes it down.*) Let's try it. See if it fits.

MARTIN   So that's all of them.

SARAH   That's all of them.

             She turns the tape off.

MARTIN   So, what have we got?

SARAH   Okay, these are all the songs, just their titles, on
             Chris's mixtape.

             I Still Remember

             First Time I Saw You

             I Can't Explain

             Everything Is Broken

             Because

             Eye Know

             From Now On

             I Am Two People

             Or

             Half A Person

             That's How I Knew This Story Would Break My
             Heart

             Side Two:

             When The World Was Young

             We Danced Together

             Even Though You Can't Dance

             MARTIN laughs. SARAH slaps him.

             I Wonder If You Know

             I Am Still Here

             Lost In Music

             I Wanna Testify

             Somewhere (There's A Place For Us)

             It's Impossible

             And

             It's All True

Coz I Luv You

Ask

Martin.

…

…

…

Well, Martin?

56

Ten years earlier. JULIA voices CHRIS's signed lines.

CHRIS   Oh God.

JULIA   It won't take long.

CHRIS   We're –

JULIA   In Sign.

CHRIS   –

JULIA   In *Sign!*

CHRIS   **I'm going out for dinner with Sarah.**

JULIA   Okay well you'd better concentrate then.

CHRIS   Okay. **Okay.**

JULIA   Promise?

CHRIS   (What's 'I promise'?)

JULIA   **I promise.**

CHRIS   Okay. **I promise.**

JULIA   <u>**Hello Chris, how are you today**</u>?

CHRIS   **Hello Julia, unfortunately I am dead.**

JULIA   Christopher!

CHRIS   **Hello Julia, unfortunately I am dead.**

JULIA   (*Resigned sigh.*)

         Oh I am sorry to hear that. How did you die?

CHRIS   **It's a very sad story, are you sure you want to hear?**

JULIA   **Yes. I like sad stories.**

CHRIS   **I was on stage at a big loud crowd in the US.**

JULIA   What's **big loud crowd?**

CHRIS   Major rock festival. **I made it up.**

JULIA   No, major rock festival is **major rock festival.**

CHRIS   **You did Rock Festivals in your evening class?**

JULIA   **No I saw it on TV.** Anyway, **you were onstage at an American rock festival.**

CHRIS   **And just as I went on stage, it started to rain.**

JULIA   **Oh dear.**

CHRIS   **And when I went up to the mike, I got a massive...**

JULIA   **Electric shock?**

CHRIS   **Yes. I got a massive electric shock.**

JULIA   **Did it hurt?**

CHRIS   **Very very very very very much. Yes.**

JULIA   **What is it like to die?**

CHRIS   …

It's very strange. Everything goes blue. And I can see for miles and miles and miles and miles and miles.

JULIA   **What do you miss about being alive?**

CHRIS   **Love and vinyl.**

JULIA   **Don't go will you?**

CHRIS   **I'm not going anywhere.**

JULIA   **Or if you do, take me too.**

CHRIS   **Sure. Okay.**

JULIA   **I wouldn't survive. Not all of me. That day at the hospital after your accident, I knew that if you died, part of me would die too.**

CHRIS   **If part of you dies**

Let's hope it's your bloody awful taste in music.

JULIA   **Bastard.**

57

At a computer.

MARTIN   There. impossiblegigs.com.

SARAH   I don't get it.

MARTIN   Reviews of gigs that never happened.

SARAH   There's hundreds of them.

MARTIN   1,273 so far.

SARAH   And none of are real?

MARTIN   Gigs that didn't happen. Gigs that wouldn't happen. Gigs that couldn't happen. He wrote about them all. He did a great review of the Jesus and Mary Chain reunion tour, but we had to pull that when they actually had a reunion tour.

SARAH   Whose idea was it?

MARTIN   All his. I just set the site up for him. He wrote everything.

SARAH   Do people read this?

MARTIN   You are number 11,764 today, look.

SARAH   You're kidding me.

MARTIN   He has fans around the world.

SARAH   I don't believe it.

MARTIN   See for yourself.

SARAH   Why do they come?

MARTIN   To be there. Finally.

SARAH   They're so detailed.

MARTIN   You should read his review of Buddy Holly at the House of Blues in 1992. He goes song by song; he tells us what Buddy's stage patter is; who was in the audience, how they reacted. Apparently Buddy Holly does a mean cover of 'Dancing in the Dark'.

SARAH   But
         Why?

MARTIN   Okay.
         Click on 1995.
         And scroll down to the Manic Street Preachers.

SARAH   Astoria. That's our gig.

MARTIN   It's the first one he did.

SARAH   But why's it on here? That gig happened. That's where we met.

MARTIN   The one where Richey smashed his guitar and Chris squeezed your hand?

SARAH   Yes.

MARTIN   You met in autumn 1995.

SARAH   So?

MARTIN   Richey disappeared in February of that year. Never seen again. Certainly not seen six months later smashing his guitar on the stage of the Astoria.

SARAH   But we were there.

MARTIN   Not in this universe you weren't.

SARAH   But it's where we met!

MARTIN   You got two evenings mixed up and you've told each other the mixed-up version so often, you can't remember what's real. It happens.

SARAH   So this review –

MARTIN   Is the first one he did. He wanted to make it real again.

SARAH   (*Reads.*) London's Astoria Theatre was once a cinema and it takes a truly widescreen band to fill this venue. Tonight's gig by The Manic Street Preachers was a classic of the genre: Nicky Wire in a dress? Check. 'Motorcycle Emptiness'? It was an epic. Eyeliner? By the bucketload. The Manics are channelling the spirit of rock 'n' roll and somehow lighting the way forward. They can revive even the most tawdry rock clichés, as when Richey Edwards, much revived from his brief sabbatical in February this year, destroyed his guitar in the blazing climax of 'You Love Us'.

And love you we do; as Richey stared hard into the crowd, who didn't feel the love curl through the room and reflect that in love as in rock 'n' roll, sometimes only a cliché will do? Tonight I am proud to say, I love you, and I always will.

SARAH   We stopped going to gigs –

MARTIN   So this was somewhere you could go to gigs together.

SARAH   There's A Place For Us
            It's Impossible
            And
            It's All True
            Coz I Luv You.

MARTIN   I would have told you about the site.
            I didn't know what was the right time.

SARAH   Why didn't he tell me?

MARTIN   I guess he has. I guess he wanted to give you the tape and let you work it out.

SARAH   He didn't know something was going to happen –

MARTIN   No. He can't have done.

SARAH   No yes.

MARTIN   I guess he was

SARAH   Yes yes.

MARTIN   You okay cos

SARAH   I'm – no actually I'm a bit...

MARTIN   You want a glass of

SARAH   It's quite a lot to, you know...

MARTIN   No no of

SARAH   I feel strange.

MARTIN   to let it all

SARAH   A pressure, here.

MARTIN   you need to do just

SARAH   Like it's going to burst out.

MARTIN   John Hurt in *Alien*, no seriou

SARAH   Too much feeling for one body or something.

MARTIN   n't catch that

SARAH   Just one body.

MARTIN   eed to shout or cry or ju

SARAH   I really don't feel right.

MARTIN   call you a doctor if

SARAH   Sorry? I'm not…

MARTIN   just an ambulance unle

SARAH   I need to lie down.

MARTIN   ook very pale are y

SARAH   Lie down.

MARTIN   alking very qu

SARAH   Do you hear that?

MARTIN   what di

SARAH   You hear that?

MARTIN   all a doc

SARAH   Agnus Dei.

MARTIN   wha

SARAH   Agnus Dei.

58

'Agnus Dei' by Rufus Wainwright, emerging from static which has built up through the end of the last scene.

From around 1'05" to near the end. We need to include the shift to the major at 4'08".

All four interpret it in some way. Maybe SARAH is separate, since this will seem to be happening inside her head.

Light, height, solemnity, majesty.

Fade to static

Which becomes the space between stations on a car radio.

Which tunes in, irregularly, to a station playing 'Strange Religion' by The Mark Lanegan Band.

59

JULIA, MARTIN, CHRIS signing for SARAH.

SARAH   A year after the funeral, I take my first trip in the car.

I want to get out of the city

Not that I have any love for the country

I want to find a place that is neither city nor country

I find the sat nav reassuring even when I am going nowhere in particular.

The sat nav seems to be looking down at the road from around 20 feet above it.

It makes me feel like I've got someone who'll watch over me.

Even though no one does, not really.

The city melts away

The suburbs thin out

Is this the country? I don't know.

Undulating hills.

Fields.

In the distance I see a figure on the brow of a hill.

Of course I recognise him immediately

The outline, the way he holds himself

I don't need to stop

I don't even need to wave

Better to keep going.

Just keep driving.

It's okay.

I have the radio on.

The car stereo grows in volume, clarifies, loses its static and fills the theatre as all goes dark.

END

CHRIS'S TAPE

Side A

1. Micah P Hinson & The Gospel Of Progress 'I Still Remember'

2. Euros Childs 'First Time I Saw You'

3. The Who 'I Can't Explain'

4. Bob Dylan 'Everything is Broken'

5. The Beatles 'Because'

6. De La Soul 'Eye Know'

7. Pavement 'From Now On'

8. Morrissey 'I Am Two People'

9. Sonic Youth 'Or'

10. The Smiths 'Half A Person'

11. Aimee Mann 'That's How I Knew This Story Would Break My Heart'

Side B

1. Billy Mackenzie 'When The World Was Young'

2. The Rakes 'We Danced Together'

3. The Raindrops 'Even Though You Can't Dance'

4. The Louvin Brothers 'I Wonder If You Know'

5. Damien Jurado 'I Am Still Here'

6. The Fall 'Lost In Music'

7. Parliament 'I Wanna Testify'

8. Tom Waits 'Somewhere (There's A Place For Us)'

9. Elvis Presley 'It's Impossible'

10. Microdisney 'And'

11. The Lemonheads 'It's All True'

12. The Smiths 'Ask'

13. Monkey Swallows the Universe 'Martin'